WITHDRAWN

DRY GARDENS

DRY GARDENS

HIGH STYLE FOR LOW WATER GARDENS

DANIEL NOLAN

Photography by Caitlin Atkinson

RIZZOLI
NEW YORK

New York · Paris · London · Milan

First published in the United States of America in 2018
by Rizzoli International Publications, Inc.
300 Park Avenue South
New York, NY 10010

www.rizzoliusa.com

Photography © 2018 Caitlin Atkinson

Designer: Su Barber
Rizzoli Editor: Martynka Wawrzyniak

2018 2019 2020 2021 / 10 9 8 7 6 5 4 3 2

Distributed in the U.S. trade by Random House,
New York

Printed in China

ISBN: 9780847861262

Library of Congress Control Number: 2018933888

A gravel staircase that is both informal and modern is the hallmark of a Terremoto landscape design. Here, a staircase leads the visitor to a hillside perch, transitioning from the planned landscape into the native surroundings.

FOREWORD

FLORA GRUBB

I came of age as a gardener during a drought in Austin, Texas, in the 90s. During that time, as I became increasingly garden-obsessed, I spent a lot of time in the city's Zilker Botanical Garden. And because I was still a teenage delinquent, I was particularly fond of scaling the fence and visiting at night when it was closed.

I adored this garden—my mother had taken me to it regularly since I was a child. It was on one of my moonlight visits that I first saw the new "xeriscape" garden that had replaced a bed of thirsty pachysandra on a patch of land near the parking lot. Knowing what I do now about public gardens, I can imagine the politics behind installing this sparse, gravelly garden with a palette of plants all at home in the Texas landscape—yuccas, salvia, dasylirions, and cacti—in an otherwise lush, water-intensive landscape full of roses and annuals.

Because I was a young gardener with a hand-watered garden, the impracticality of the water-intensive annuals that I experimented with was soon made clear to me. And because I had been raised to take short showers and turn off the water while I brushed my teeth or lathered my hands,

I was appalled by the amount of water I had to dump on thirsty annuals and the scruffy little lawn I had inherited just to keep them alive in the heat of summer. I quickly abandoned them for less thirsty options. I've been completely committed to gardens that use less water ever since, and I brought my water-conserving habits with me when I embarked upon a career in gardening in the Bay Area.

I still hold in my heart a deep love for the rambling, romantic Zilker Botanical Garden, with its waterfalls, Japanese moon bridge, and dripping wisteria, and, as a nurserywoman, I have set out to conjure that same love throughout my career by choosing to work with plants that demand fewer resources.

Those of us who think deeply about gardens and care deeply about the environment must champion the creation of gardens that suit every taste yet inspire the gardening public to conserve water. We must continue to create romantic, extravagant, dramatic gardens that are "dry" only in the sense that they use less water. As you will see in the following pages, when you design gardens that are light on the land, you sacrifice nothing in the way of style.

Daniel Nolan is among my favorite garden designers because of his unflinching commitment to beautiful, romantic gardens. In this book, Daniel has scoured America for gardens that seduce and enchant, collecting them into a gorgeous compendium with his exacting eye.

Seasoned by his work designing and planting gardens in Pennsylvania's Brandywine Valley, South Carolina, Los Angeles, and here in the San Francisco Bay Area, Daniel makes using less water a feature—not a nuisance—of creating gardens that satisfy our deepest joys. The conspicuously dry garden is not the topic of this book, but the high-style garden that enriches the land and our lives.

Ultimately, making, tending, and living with a beautiful garden that takes less water also gratifies our deep need to tend to our greater world. Daniel inspires me—and I hope you—to picture the joyful and consequential possibilities that making dry gardens opens.

A striking combination of silver torch cacti (*Cleistocactus strausii*), gray elephant ear (*Kalanchoe beharensis*) and yellow African candelabra (*Euphorbia ammak* 'Variegata') create interest and texture in Judy Kameon's Los Angeles garden for French fashion brand Balenciaga.

Photo: Tom Mannion

INTRODUCTION

DANIEL NOLAN

I can recall the exact moment when I became interested in drought-tolerant gardens. It was 2011, and I'd opened *The New York Times Magazine* to a stunning spread of the garden in front of Balenciaga's Los Angeles store. It took my breath away. Sculpture-like white cacti poked out of black basalt gravel, geometric pavers created a walkway, and in the background were giant green birds-of-paradise and a few soft gray *Kalanchoes*. It altered my perception of what a garden could be, and it made me think about what we choose as our criteria of what makes a garden. It had scale, texture, and it embraced the positive and negative spaces so clearly. It was a revelation to me.

Since that moment, I have designed gardens that combine the spirit of drought tolerance with design. It's not always cactus and plants that people commonly associate with "drought," it's also the reimagining of a space without the typical American-sized lawn. When a 100-square-foot lawn requires 62 gallons of water annually, and many states are restricting irrigation use due to drought or water conservation, we should be looking at ways to reduce the resources and energy our personal spaces consume.

When approaching new projects, I will commonly ask myself, "Is there a way we can reduce the water consumption?" It can be done by reducing the size of a lawn, expanding the hardscape, selecting a hardier groundcover, or selecting plants and trees that can survive long periods of time without significant water. If a project requires not an overhaul but a gentle hand, I consider leaving a mature specimen that has already established itself into the site and frame it with plants that won't interfere with its watering cycle or widen the beds to accommodate more of a drought-tolerant plant palette.

The concept of a drought is not universal—in some regions, droughts last months; in others, they can last years. For instance, conditions in the American South—where droughts do take place but the water table can still remain high—create a different set of issues for gardeners than in the Southwest, where there is a never-ending demand for water, so plant material must be able to adapt to short periods of rain. What connects these locations is the vision to use plants that are adaptable and appropriate for each region's water availability and to utilize them in a design sense where they achieve maximum graphic impact, enhancing the senses in a different way from most traditional gardens. These gardens challenge the common perception still so prevalent in garden culture, that gardens are mainly for flowers or edible use. There is a growing number of landscape architects that are embracing this new way to design water-conscious gardens, as well as a community of people who commission these projects.

I think as we continue to design more of these gardens and spaces, the culture will begin to change more quickly. People will ask for more of these plants, increasing the volume of drought-tolerant material in garden stores. They will reconsider existing thirstier plant selections in their gardens and lawns, and new projects will incorporate an increase of native plants and more efficient and strategic irrigation systems. It's been a slow but steady transition. The garden world is quick to embrace trends but not movements, so every time I can convince a client to choose an agave over a rose, it's a small victory.

WEST

SONOMA HILL TOP
ARTERRA LANDSCAPE ARCHITECTS
SONOMA, CALIFORNIA

Some of the most successful gardens are not about man's control over nature, but instead, how man responds respectfully to his surroundings. Perched on a hilltop that overlooks the Sonoma Valley, amid the forest of manzanitas and redwoods, this home's open plan is designed to catch the commanding views, not impede them. Native and drought-tolerant grasses, mixed with olives and *Arctostaphylos manzanita*, are planted against the home and blend seamlessly into the fields, intentionally blurring the line between wild and planned. The pool—situated at the edge of the hill—reflects its border of tall grasses, which directs the viewer's eye out to the valley and beyond. An atmosphere of tranquility prevails throughout the property—there appears nothing to prune or clip. Here, the wilderness has nearly returned to the front doorsteps, asking nothing more than to be viewed and left alone.

This home, designed by Bay Area architects Feldman Architecture, blurs the lines between inside and outside, using oversized glass panels that rise toward the ceiling, turning the building into an outdoor pavilion.

Logging in the 1800s degraded the 40-acre site, and invasive species moved in. Arterra's mission was to restore and revitalize the property with native grasses, and allow the land to heal itself.

SAN ANSELMO RESIDENCE
LUTSKO ASSOCIATES
SAN ANSELMO, CALIFORNIA

Quietly reflecting on the mountains in the distance, this home garden's power is in the subtle touches of form and shape, as well as its masterful framing of the breathtaking views in all directions. Designed by Bay Area landscape architect Ron Lutsko, the garden is relatively small in scale—just under half an acre—but makes up for its size with a deft plant selection and placement. In harmony with the muted tones of the surrounding Marin County landscape, which consists of a balance of thick fog and blazing sun, often appearing both in the same day, the garden's masses of santolinas, punctuated by *Arbutus* 'Marina,' are the perfect counterpoint to the sculptural San Pedro cacti and prickly pears, which rise against the home's exterior. It's the expert balance of arid and Mediterranean that gives this this garden an ethereal, yet modern, mood.

"The design intent for this residence was to augment the site's natural surroundings, create a retreat from its suburban context, and achieve a level of privacy that invites indoor/outdoor living."

—Ron Lutsko

A simple container garden is not so simple. Mexican giant cardon (*Pachycereus pringlei*) and Indian corn cob (*Euphorbia mammillaris var. variegata*) are surrounded here by potted golden barrel cacti (*Echinocactus grusonii*).

The perfect balance of soft pink muhly grass (*Muhlenbergia capillaris*) hangs over a planting of tall San Pedro cacti (*Echinopsis pachanoi*) and violet pricklypear (*Opuntia gosseliniana*).

BERNAL HEIGHTS RESIDENCE
DANIEL NOLAN DESIGN
SAN FRANCISCO, CALIFORNIA

San Francisco is known for stunning gardens, and their creators are not afraid to push the limits of design. When a low-key couple bought their new home on a quiet street, which is situated against a scenic city park, they decided they wanted to push the envelope as far it could go and create a show-stopping collection of plants from around the world. This collection of strange and unusual plants is a knockout, with species selected more for their intriguing botanical history than their decorative qualities. Cacti from the Atlas Mountains mingle next to terrestrial bromeliads from the heights of the Andes; and trees from the Australian bush are tucked in among vibrant leucadendrons from South Africa—and this is just the front yard, The backyard is a prehistoric jungle—leafy, lush, and all green, then punctuated by cacti and agaves. It's the client's personal botanical garden, shared with curious neighbors, and the City by the Bay.

A screen of silver torch
cacti (*Cleistocactus
strausii*) is visible
from the front door;
in the back garden
are octopus agave
(*Agave vilmoriniana*).

The rear garden is steep and contains heavy clay soil, so plants like the giant white bird of paradise (*Strelitzia Nicolai*) and pygmy date palm (*Phoenix roebelenii*) were planted above the garden in order to catch water coming down the hill during periods of rain.

MID PENINSULA GARDEN
DANIEL NOLAN DESIGN
MENLO PARK, CALIFORNIA

First impressions are everything. Behind a gate, off a busy street, and up a narrow driveway shaded by mature oaks, is a garden with a planting combination that lets the guest know immediately upon arrival that the homeowners are not afraid to make a statement. The front yard, comprised of sculptural succulent *Furcraea macdougalii* that rise out of a bed of blue agaves, and a carpet of yellow sedums, sets the tone for the entire site. The garden's plantings appear so balanced with the proportions of the home that just a quick look around the property and the visitor knows instantly that nothing was left to chance. It is surprising to learn that the clients were initially cautious when the work first started in 2011. The project began small, with the replanting of a modest-sized bed. This then led to a larger bed in the backyard, and soon, the entire property was overhauled to accommodate a bocce court, outdoor entertaining area, a reduction of the lawn's original footprint to accommodate for more plants, and a widening of the existing beds to make room for a large gravel bed for the palms. The end result is magic—a layered and cohesive planting that manages to be exuberant and sophisticated at the same time.

Clockwise, from top left: *Agave* 'Blue Glow' underplanted with *Sedum rupestre* 'Angelina'; a pair of date palms (*Phoenix dactylifera*); a sunken bocce court filled with crushed oyster shells; a quiet corner of the garden.

"I think the role of a garden designer is to interpret the desires of a client, though most client's think they know what they want only because they are familiar ideas. Challenging those notions in the design process and taking a lighter hand when necessary may not be every designer's primary concern, but it works for me."

—Daniel Nolan

Spiky *Furcraea
macdougalii* announce
the front door.
Opposite: The built-in
wraparound planter
containing conebush
(*Leucadendron* 'Safari
Sunset') and kangaroo
paw (*Anigozanthos*'
Orange Cross') explodes
with warmth in an
otherwise cool garden.

CARMEL CLIFF HOUSE
RON MANN DESIGN
CARMEL, CALIFORNIA

There are countless modern homes by talented architects, but there are only a handful of homes designed by true artists. A home that blends the interior and exterior beautifully and with such care that one can tell immediately that the exterior plants were selected specifically for their forms and textures just as the building's materials were. Positioning the home around the property's existing stately oaks, then creating integrated planters to house them meant that the architect, Ron Mann, had to carefully observe the land and its views before a single hole was dug or nail was hammered. This attention to detail and careful consideration of the plants becomes more astounding upon learning that Ron is not a landscape designer but an artist who creates custom homes, furniture, and artwork. The minimal-planting palette shows the designer's restraint—soft agaves protrude from the rocks like coral branches, palms trunks soar like columns, and philodendron leaves drape over walls, all suggesting a lushness that counters the home's brutal concrete forms.

All the furniture was custom designed by home and garden designer Ron Mann. *Tillandsia xerographica,* an air plant that thrives on cool mist and blasts of sunshine, makes an arresting centerpiece when arranged *en masse.*

Clockwise, from top left: Life-size terracotta figures stand guard; Mediterranean fan palms (*Chamaerops humilis*) in the corner planter; fox tail agaves (*Agave attenuate*) reach out of a rocky bed; poolside custom chaise lounges.

Green *Agave salmiana* mixed with gray century plants (*Agave americana*) stud the hillside behind native oaks and punctuate the hardscape that leads to the front of the home.

"I get help from the greatest designer: Mother Nature. Design is a reflection of the world around us and also creates the world."

—Ron Mann

Angled planters contain mass plantings of *Philodendron selloum* and Black Bamboo (*Phyllostachys nigra*) to shield and soften the home's massive size.

LOS PALMAS ESTATE
STEVE MARTINO LANDSCAPE
ARCHITECTS
PALM SPRINGS, CALIFORNIA

It seems almost cliché, the Palm Springs vernacular of the low-slung midcentury ranch home, punctuated by palms, its plan centered around the pool. Then there is the garden—created by Steve Martino, it upends this assumption and makes you reconsider the boundaries of resort style. Blending arid with lush, cacti borders surround the house against cool stucco walls and are densely planted yet curated, striking combinations placed as deliberately as brush strokes on a canvas. The cacti lead you to the backyard, where towering grey and green palm fronds carry the neutral-toned balance of plants into the sky. Beneath them, vertical forms of cacti follow suit, making the garden feel alive and electric and all without a bloom in site. Though the path of lawn is postage-stamp sized, the coolness of the space feels almost spa-like, and in the blazing heat of the day it invites guests to remain inside its walls as if the bustle of the outside world doesn't exist.

Mexican blue palms (*Brahea armata*) rise from the pool. Opposite: Black-spined agave (*Agave macroacantha*), barrel cactus (*Echinocactus grussonii*), and beaked yucca (*Yucca rostrate*) make a striking combination.

Palm Springs lives up to its name: Mexican blue palms (*Brahea armata*) in the foreground, date palms (*Phoenix dactylifera*), and Mexican fan palm (*Washingtonia robusta*) in the rear create layers of texture and height against the sky.

SADDLE PEAK
SANT ARCHITECTS
LOS ANGELES, CALIFORNIA

Driving through the winding Topanga Canyon, with every turn narrower than the last, a quick turn off the road leads you right into a dead end—a giant boulder to be exact. However, moving beyond the massive rock is like a curtain being lifted from a stage. A pathway leads to a garden and natural courtyard, revealing a spectacular home perched on a Malibu mountaintop. Brilliantly set, the home has been oriented for a perfect view to watch the daily sun set into the Pacific. In the surrounding garden, the necks of *Agave attenuata* emerge from the ground as if straining to catch the last glimpse of light. The native scrub of pine and oak blend with soft grey acacias and deep red arbutus trunks, which also shield the house from views of neighboring homes; and a covering of pale brown gravel blends so seamlessly with the natural tones of the hillside that it feels as if the garden extends deep down into the canyons below and out into the horizon.

A Cootamundra wattle (*Acacia baileyana*) provides a silvery blue screen of privacy, and fox tail agaves (*Agave attenuata*) dot the hillside.

Clockwise, from top left: Fox tail agaves (*Agave attenuates*) patiently turn toward the sun; the pool's backdrop is a dramatic boulder, set between the guest house and the main home. Opposite: The view coming around the massive boulder toward the main home.

BEL AIR ANZIO
TERREMOTO
LOS ANGELES, CALIFORNIA

The team at Terremoto vividly explored the line between control and chaos when designing this residential garden in the hills of Bel Air. The impressive, bright-white, ultra-contemporary home stands in stark contrast with the surrounding hillside that is covered with rambling perennials and grasses, punctuated with agaves. The tension is dynamic; the property has multiple areas for entertaining and relaxing, all connected by angled boardwalks and steep stairs. The garden is athletic, robust, and unpretentious, yet seems to thrive on the attention of guests who often migrate from the sunken pool to the seating around the fireplace and then the lawn. It's clear that nothing goes to waste in this garden—its energy almost palpable, encouraging adventure and play.

A quiet scene over-looking the garden. Opposite: Western sycamores (*Platanus racemosa*) above a pathway filled with drought-tolerant autumn moor grass (*Sesleria autumnalis*) and Salvias.

On the hillside, blue Magellan wheat grass (*Elymus magellanicus*) with scented blue sage (*Salvia clevelandii*) and silver grass (*Miscanthus*) control erosion and create a blanket of color and texture.

A sculptural Olive tree (*Olea wilsonii*) underplanted with hairawn muhly (*Muhlenbergia capillaris*) and century plants (*Agave Americana*) greet visitors at the front entrance of the home. Opposite: Custom furniture is arranged around the outdoor fireplace, centering the gardening and providing a source of warmth when darkness falls.

"We've created an office that's all about tearing down and mixing up horticultural tropes, and I don't think we could do that as recklessly on the East Coast as we can here in California. Though, it's sometimes a shame that the gardening scene in Los Angeles is not very robust; but, what that allows are greater opportunities for botanical anarchy. We can do as we please—because who is to judge us?"

—David Godshall

BEL AIR ESTATE
LISA GIMMY LANDSCAPE ARCHITECTURE
LOS ANGELES, CALIFORNIA

Patience is perhaps the most important characteristic for a garden designer, and maybe even more so for the client. When this patience is exercised and the need for immediate gratification is delayed, a garden can mature and develop on its own at its own pace. It's thrilling to see these gardens grow into maturity; the weak ideas can be abandoned when, over time, the garden's key elements are in place. Today, this garden is as masterful and confident as it was in 2005, when it was designed and installed by Lisa Gimmy after the owner—who was uninspired by his home's 3,700-square-foot grass lawn—contacted her for the task of creating a stylized, low-water garden. The front yard offers massive *Dasylirion longissimum* and agaves, their trunks poking out of beds of fountain grass, or *Pennisetum fescue*. The backyard is a collector's garden of aloes and succulents, which rest behind a zigzagging hedge of *Teucrium chamaedrys*, giving the garden the feel that it's floating above the hills of Bel Air.

Aloes, agaves, and dracaenas all mix together to give the front garden a sculptural feel. Opposite: slipper plants (*Pedilanthus bracteatus*) and potted pencil cacti (*Euphorbia tirucalli*) frame the entrance to the backyard.

Mexican grass trees (*Dasylirion longissimum*), native to Northeast Mexico, are perfect for catching the light of the setting sun. Underplanted with blue fescue grasses (*Festuca glauca*), they become equal parts soft and striking.

"Californians, generally speaking, understand that the days of the front-yard lawn are coming to an end. But what's confusing to the general public is that 'what's next' in regards to the residential landscape can be about a hundred different things."

—Terremoto

HANCOCK PARK HIDEAWAY
ADAM SIRAK
LOS ANGELES, CALIFORNIA

To cohesively combine the influential styles of Morocco and West Texas seems inconceivable, so maybe it's fitting that in Los Angeles, where anything is possible, this small garden proves the two looks are a perfect marriage. The curated collection of desert plants in rustic terracotta containers evoke the vibe of a rooftop garden in Marrakesh, while the garden's materials—gravel, bamboo, a covered pergola, and board-formed concrete—are also decidedly rugged and could have been sourced straight from the Lone Star State. The whole space is expertly put to use, with the entertaining area off the kitchen, a picnic table shaded by vines, and multiple areas to lay down and relax. One can imagine spending the entire weekend in the backyard, dipping in the shallow pool, soaking up the sun, reading in the hammock, and enjoying a drink under the loggia. This garden isn't just for moving through—it almost demands the visitor slow down and relax in its cool ambiance.

A collection of cacti, all coordinated in terracotta containers, provide a graphic element under the loggia. Opposite: The collection continues as beaked yucca (*Yucca rostrata*) and Snowy River wattle (*Acacia boormanii*) provide height and scale to the garden.

Clockwise, from top left: The garden seen through the master bedroom; muted tones extend the space; a cacti collection; the outdoor seating area is both informal and refined.

HERMOSA PROJECT
JONES LANDSCAPES
LOS ANGELES, CALIFORNIA

Life at the beach can seem a little slow paced, but this garden works overtime. In the quiet neighborhood of Hermosa Beach, South Bay firm Jones Landscapes teamed up with Pepé Studio to design a garden that would blur the lines between inside and outside. The use of mostly Australian and South African plants were a natural fit for this location, not only because the homeowners hail from South Africa but also because these species are well adapted to handling harsh coastal weather conditions. With the Pacific Ocean just steps from the front door, the exterior garden is set to handle the back-and-forth of guests and children without showing any wear. The interior has a more intimate setting, with a central courtyard that includes a sunken spa, accessible through sliding glass doors. The brilliant use of bamboo, dracaenas, and *Philodendron selloum* are as low maintenance as they come—perfect for a busy family enjoying the Southern California lifestyle.

Just a few steps from the beach, the home is open to the elements. Opposite: *Agave* 'Blue Flame' and Australian rosemary (*Westringia fruticosa*) create the ideal blend of form and texture.

100

The discreet plan of the floor-level hot tub creates visual interest and doesn't distract from the serenity of the space. Opposite: A triangle ficus (*Ficus triangularis*) brings the exterior inside.

Walls of sliding glass doors allow light and air to permeate the home. Opposite: Dwarf olives (*Olea europaea 'Montra'*) and succulents mixed with Mexican feathergrass (*Stipa tenuissima*) soften the board-formed concrete walls and greet visitors at the front pathway.

PHOENIX OASIS
COLWELL SHELOR
PARADISE VALLEY, ARIZONA

The team at Colwell Shelor has used the limited space of this private suburban home to their advantage, creating a garden with a jewel box effect. The lush, densely packed, sculptural plants offset by the home's ample windows create a composition that invites the eye outdoors but also brings the garden inside. As with many homes in the Southwest, the home is situated around the pool—from where the entertaining and lounging radiates—and its reflective surface is a mirror for the surrounding plants. The pool's spiky garden of succulents and cacti gives way to the lush, weeping Mexican bamboo positioned behind the fire pit area, creating a soft curtain of foliage. Amid the dense plantings, there is a single bed reserved for two sculptural cacti, placed squarely in the center; surrounded by red stone as if pieces of art or specimens plucked from the surface of another planet. A lone palo verde tree sits in the adjacent bed, single and solitary, its green trunk is reflected in the pool's waters. The appeal of the garden is twofold: the rich combination of plants and grasses create a backdrop of interest and texture; and the restraint of the beds closest to the home help create context and scale, making it easy to take in the space as whole.

Agaves, aloes,
grasses, and cacti
combine to create
a jewel box garden.
Opposite: A circular
pad is semi-enclosed
to create privacy
as well interesting
graphics interest.

"Cactus thorns in the early morning light are simply breathtaking—the way they glow, and how you can see every fine detail of the needle, like thorns in their protective skin. They remind us of the beauty in such a harsh environment. We want our clients to experience those simple moments in their landscape."

—Michele Shelor

DESERT RETREAT
THE GARDEN GATE
MARANA, ARIZONA

A modern, concrete home situated in a valley outside Tuscon is the setting for a sculptural garden that lays lightly on the land, willfully calling attention to its dramatic surroundings. The idea was not to distract from the site's rugged natural beauty, so a restrained palette of plants that look as if they came directly from the hills was used to soften the edges. The gardens leading to the house almost replicate the landscape before the home was built, with cacti and yuccas closely approaching the walkways. Against the house, single species—mostly planted in large drifts to avoid calling too much attention—create solid bands of color and lead the eye around the space and out into the valley beyond. The pool is the main focus but not in the way one would imagine. Rectangular in shape, it faces the opening of the valley and is offset by a square base with a steel, cage-like box rising from its platform, creating another window to view the valley. The home almost doesn't feel landscaped, which is one of the great qualities of a good landscape design; the garden embraces its surroundings and then puts the house into that setting. This is a magical space, built with a quality that few gardens actually achieve.

CLOS PEGASE WINERY
DANIEL NOLAN DESIGN
NAPA, CALIFORNIA

Located in the northern end of Napa Valley, the Clos Pegase Winery garden redesign was no small task—it not only needed to speak to its setting and history but also had to stand up to the commanding building by iconic postmodern architect, Michael Graves. In 2015, at the height of California's drought, the garden—which was then a single lawn—was replaced with a variety of plant species from various Mediterranean-like climates, including rarities like Australian grass trees—*Xanthorrhoea preissii*—and critically threatened Chilean wine palm, *Jubaea chilensis*. The garden is comprised of two elements: the "rooms," which lead off from the building, and the two cactus gardens, which bookend the rooms. The rooms have fruitless olives in each corner and a ring of white benches in the center, which provide a space for shaded contemplation or conversation. The gardens at each end are meant to inspire a curiosity of the botanical world, with agaves, cacti, yuccas, and *Acacia baileyana* planted en masse. But the crowning achievement of the garden is the 19 leafy *Jubaea chilensis*—the largest public planting north of Santa Barbara—whose smooth trunks will soon match the size and scale of the building's main pillar. The gardens mindfully compliment the Winery, taking in its size and presence and replying with careful and deliberate exuberance.

Sawblade (*Dyckia* 'Grape Jelly') sends up long-lasting orange flowers at the base of the San Pedro cactus (*Echinopsis pachanoi*). Opposite: Towering spikes of the desert spoon (*Dasylirion wheeleri*) flank the entrance to the winery.

SCRIBE WINERY
TERREMOTO
SONOMA, CALIFORNIA

Some do not naturally see the romance of the drought-tolerant aesthetic, but a visit to Scribe Winery in the foothills of Sonoma will convert even the most reluctant. The experience begins as you are led up a driveway lined with mature palms, which subtly reinforce the order of the vineyards that surround on both sides. The winery's charming farmhouse lies at the top of the driveway, and its gardens ramble down the side, perfumed by *Salvia clevelandii*, artemisias, and rosemary, mixed with grasses and California lilacs. It's these uniquely contrasting combinations that enchant—the dark lavender of the prickly pear next to the white roses and tan grasses. A mix of dusky colors and tactile textures invite you to deeply inhale their scent and linger for hours on the patio, perhaps with a glass of wine, as you watch the sun slowly set in the distance.

"I love gardens that have been abandoned or forgotten—they aren't clipped and pruned to death, and anything needing such care is long gone. I hope that is the future of gardens—the human desire for control and order has fallen away, and the plants are free to grow at their own pace."

— Daniel Nolan

TONGVA PARK
JAMES CORNER FIELD OPERATIONS
SANTA MONICA, CALIFORNIA

It's hard to imagine that Tongva Park, located next to the famed Santa Monica Pier, was once an underused parking lot. Opened in 2013, the 6-acre property, designed by James Corner Field Operations of New York City's High Line fame, now boasts winding paths lined with palms, ficus, and other exotic species. The park also hosts a masterful plant selection of agaves, aloes, and drought-tolerant grasses—170 unique species in all. The result is a botanical garden that is also a recreational park, where two central areas of grass are enclosed by dense and drought-tolerant plants, which roll and spill down a lightly-raised topography created to mimic hills, a welcomed feature to the previous flat property. Another key feature is the single channel of water that almost cuts the space in half, a reminder of the location's once-wild canyonscape. Though all things flow toward the ocean, the landscape here temps visitors to linger a little longer.

135

A combination of hardy palms: dwarf palmetto (*Sabal minor*), Mediterranean fan palm (*Chamaerops cerifera*), and Canary Island date palm (*Phoenix canariensis*). Opposite: Grass guru John Greenlee's masterful touch is evident in his ability to use soft seslerias and fescues to ground the park's sculpture Weather Field No. 1 by Iñigo Manglano-Ovalle.

A pindo palm (*Butia capitate*) creates a fountain-like effect amid plantings of giant tree aloe, agaves, and grasses. Opposite: A captivating blend of palms and grasses create softness and scale in the middle of Santa Monica's urban center.

"Greater societal and botanical consciousness is in motion, largely as a result of a wider acknowledgement of the importance of native landscapes in ecology. But with it also comes the necessity to change our fundamental notions of landscape and beauty. We at Terremoto enjoy horticultural collisions and the blurring of worlds. We'd like to see native gardening collide with ornamental gardens; desert gardens become Japanese. We want botanical diffusion at a global scale."

—David Godshall

ISABEL MARANT
ELYSIAN LANDSCAPES
LOS ANGELES, CALIFORNIA

How bold is clothing designer Isabel Marant to not entice passersby with large windows displaying her latest collections? Instead, she employs stalagmites of cacti, enveloped by soft-grey *Kalanchoe beharensis*, and punctuated by agaves to lure people inside. The postcard-sized garden is an oasis in the middle of a street where store front after store front visually bombard you so much that one suffers from commercialism fatigue. But here, there is no sign or logo, just a simple pathway that leads you off the sidewalk, through a garden, and into the store—a 20-foot journey that immediately refreshes the visitor before setting a foot inside. And what a garden! Its forms and shapes have not a single flower or bloom, but, instead, color and texture. There are no surprises—in this meditative space, the plants inform that the designer isn't interested in gimmicks or tricks, but a timeless aesthetic.

"In the future, I think more gardens will be shared spaces. There will be a greater need for communal and public gardens as the world becomes more populated and private gardens become less attainable. And, as the temperatures rise, we will need more trees for shade. Hopefully we will increase our green spaces so everyone has a garden or park where they can go to connect with others, the four seasons, and nature."

—Judy Kameon

A lyrical composition of plants in similar tones, from the velvety leaves of the elephant ear (*Kalanchoe beharensis*) to the perfect symmetry of the artichoke agave (*Agave parryi var. truncata*), are punctuated with vertical columns of San Pedro cacti (*Echinopsis pachanoi*).

MOHAWK WEST
TERREMOTO
LOS ANGELES, CALIFORNIA

When the design studio Terremoto was given a blank canvas, they saw an opportunity to create an art gallery. For them, a simple garden at Santa Monica's Mohawk General Store would have been too obvious a solution. The boutique's carefully curated items and displays were Terremoto's inspiration behind the resulting mindful and artful composition. Opening off of the shop, the garden invites shoppers to take a break and venture outside to view the plants from all angles as they would sculptures in a gallery. A visit to the store's garden at different times of day reveal details of plants that even the most discerning eye might miss in one single visit. And at night, the plants are lit to create an otherworldly effect, like a garden on Mars. But even as a momentary break from retail therapy, the garden's effect is transporting and imaginative, leaving the visitor ready to return to the store for another browse, and then home, with an abundance of inspiration to design their own home garden.

The work of sculptor Ryosuke Yazaki seems to be in communication with the Mexican giant cardon (*Pachycereus pringlei*). Opposite: A tree aloe (*Aloidendron barberae*) spreads it's branches overhead while green and yellow African candelabra (*Euphorbia ammak*) boldly stand against a white wall.

The garden features many areas to sit and reflect, from a corner filled with fox tail agave (*Agave attenuate*) and dune aloe (*Aloe thraskii*) to a seat under the soaring leaves of the giant white bird of paradise (*Strelitzia nicolai*).

Yellow sandstone blocks and grey concrete offer a muted palette; the two tones are from decomposed granite found in the surrounding landscape and subtly reinforce the themes from the home's materials in the garden.

SOUTH

OLMOS PARK PROJECT
LAKE FLATO
SAN ANTONIO, TEXAS

One can almost imagine the initial garden-planning conversation between the architect and client for of this home. The rows of barrel cacti, agaves, and yuccas are laid out in perfect lines surrounding the house, suggesting the designer's sheer control and attention to detail of the site. The plants are placed in strict compositional bands to reinforce the severity of the home's architectural lines, and, throughout the project, the plant's soft blue tones play off the home's yellow sandstone walls. Giant oaks punctuate the space, creating umbrella-like canopies over the open areas, their thick, dark trucks complementing the gold gravel underneath. The effect is a masterful study of plants used conceptually as color blocks.

The home is situated around the property's sprawling oaks (*Quercus robur*), and the beds extend off the home as a grid. Each bed contains a collection of golden barrel cacti (*Echinocactus grusonii*), whale's tongue agave (*Agave ovatifolia*), and beaked yucca (*Yucca rostrata*).

LOS BALCONES
MARK WORD DESIGN
AUSTIN, TEXAS

Less is more, and in the case of the garden designed by Mark Word, less meant eliminating a full lawn in exchange for a stunning collection of low-water perennials and groundcovers. Bands of CorTen steel comprise the front steps of the home, which are filled with an impressive array of spineless prickly pear and evergreen groundcovers. It's a simplified palette, planted en masse to achieve maximum impact against the expansive concrete backdrop. The backyard integrates native boulders into a softscape of tan gravel, and its hillside is a painterly but expressive collection of succulents, grasses, agaves, and perennials, which flower over and over. It's a confident planting design, complementing and not competing with the home's bold style.

Mixed within grasses and trailing groundcover, spineless prickly pear cacti (*Opuntia cacanapa 'Ellisiana'*) greet visitors at the front door.

"The American West has always offered the luxury of space, and space often grants us some measure of freedom to do what we please. But even in small, shared courtyards, I think people in the West favor creative expression, even at the risk of functionality, which might be a direct result of the 'newness' associated with the West Coast."

—Mark Word

NEW ORLEANS MID-CENTURY
LEE LEDBETTER
NEW ORLEANS, LOUISIANA

The architect Lee Ledbetter has always had a keen eye for design. While growing up, Ledbetter's grandparents lived just three houses down from the modernist masterpiece that he now calls home; the residence was built in 1963 by New Orleans native Nathanial Curtis, who was also the architect of the New Orleans Superdome. When Ledbetter purchased the home in 2013, he decided to remain loyal to mid-century provenance on the interior. However, for the outside, he dared to eschew the typical subtropical plant palette and employ a garden that mixes cacti, succulents, and natives that thrive in the hot and humid climate. The property uses native Yaupon hollies for both sculptural tree elements and boxwood alternatives, as their low-water needs allows them to thrive in the sandy soil and withstand the area's punishing heat. Floor-to-ceiling windows bring the outside in; and each wing of the house overlooks its own courtyard, where containers filled with yuccas, furcraeas, and succulents create sculptural moments that play off the whitewashed brick. The courtyards evoke a gallery feel, perfect for a homeowner with such exacting tastes.

"I'm drawn to the sense of repose that can result from the melding of classicism/modernism with the inside/outside. In that vein, I reinforced the architecture of our living room courtyard with a balanced seating arrangement and a narrow color palette of evergreen trees, topiaries, and succulents."

—Lee Ledbetter

Clockwise, from top left: Potted century plant (*Agave americana*); clipped yaupon (*Ilex vomitoria*) is a low water topiary; a bowl full of the succulent *Haworthia*; a monstera (*Monstera deliciosa*) fills a corner.

Spikes of (*Furcraea foetida* 'Variegata') and dwarf palmettos (*Sabal minor*) counter the rounded shapes in the containers. Opposite: Most of the dry, soil-loving plants are kept in containers to promote good drainage.

JOHNS ISLAND
JIM SMEAL + ALEJANDRO GONZALEZ
CHARLESTON, SOUTH CAROLINA

What do cactus-loving gardeners do when they live steps from the water in coastal South Carolina? They mound their beds with loamy, fast-draining soil, and plant agaves, yuccas, and dyckias in broad swathes with abandon. The home gardeners expertly added in *Ilex vomitoria*, or Yaupon holly, as an olive branch to the local style, which is often more traditional, where camellias are picked before cacti. In addition, a patch of lawn was replaced with beds of lomandras and yuccas, which happily tap into the area's high water table but never need more than an occasional watering during the hottest months. The result is a stunning garden of low-water plants that thrives under live oaks dripping with Spanish moss on a marsh off the Ashley River.

Agave angustifolia 'Marginata,' is commonly called the Caribbean agave, possibly due in part to its tolerance of the heavy rains and heat in its native habitat of Mexico and Central America.

Clumps of dyckia tie together the surrounding clipped hollies (*Ilex*) and agaves. Opposite: Beds of evergreen beaked yucca (*Yucca rostrata*) and dwarf mat rush (*Lomandra longifolia* 'Breeze') create a meadow effect that leads towards the water.

PECKERWOOD GARDEN
JOHN FAIREY
HOUSTON, TEXAS

Founded in 1971 by artist John Gaston Fairey, the Peckerwood Garden—situated 40 miles from Houston—has gone through a series of radical changes. The first was in 1983, when the property was forced into a massive overhaul after a tornado tore through its 39 acres. The burgeoning plantsman, however, saw this necessary rebuilding as an opportunity to begin experimenting with rare plants. It wasn't until 1988, during a plant-collecting trip to Northern Mexico with fellow Texan plantsman Lynn Lowery, that Fairey was struck with a new appreciation for unusual and drought-tolerant species. Over one hundred plant-collecting trips later, his garden has grown and flourished. Furthermore, Fairey has created a laboratory that provides studies for these plants, as well as species from Asia and the US, including many of which are rare or have disappeared entirely from the wild. Now the garden is included into the National Garden Conservancy, which, by law, protects it for conservation and design.

"This is my first dry garden, seen from the perspective of my old kitchen window. That house is gone, and now the garden can only be seen by going off the beaten path. The design—which I agonized over—has transitioned over time, filling in, getting bigger than expected, morphing into unintentional compositions its own. The majority of cacti here are seedlings off of just one, which I collected on my first trip to Mexico."

—John Fairey

Columns of beaked yucca (*Yucca rostrata*) are placed in heaped, decomposed granite to emphasize the building's front entrance. Opposite: Great masses of the native saw palmetto (*Serenoa repens*) are treated as a specimen in the garden.

ALYS BEACH COMMUNITY
DUANY PLATER ZYBERK
ALYS BEACH, FLORIDA

There are no shortages of planned communities on the Florida coast, but with its Bermuda-inspired architecture and carefully regulated plant selections, Alys Beach is both inspirational and aspirational. The community's 2004 master plan, created by developer Duany Plater Zyberk, calls for native plants whenever possible and requires a careful plant review before any parcel of the property is developed. Swathes of native *Sabal minor*, hollies, and grasses create cohesion and are punctuated by allées of date palms. To limit the water consumption on the property, turf is limited to public areas only, and *Arachis glabrata*—an uncommon species and member of the peanut family—is used as a drought-tolerant groundcover. Alys Beach lives up to its self-designated motto of "simplify, simplify" by planting en masse, not relying on flowering plants, and letting the plants complement the property's astounding architectural and natural surroundings.

Clockwise, from top left: Potted Chinese windmill palm (*Trachycarpus fortunei*); the foliage of dwarf palmetto (*Sabal minor*); the normally aggressive trumpet vine (*Campsis radicans*) is controlled here in raised planters; perennial peanut grass (*Arachis glabrata*) is a commonly used groundcover on the property.

The stately pindo palm (*Butia capitata*) complement the architecture of the pool area, while the native slash pine (*Pinus elliottii*) and hollies (*Ilex*) are encouraged to thrive among the Bermuda-style whitewashed homes.

Dwarf palmetto (*Sabal minor*) and low-growing junipers (*Juniperus*) create informal hedges that lead out to the beach. Opposite: Century plants (*Agave americana*) planted en masse in raised beds are used to create a dramatic effect.

Silver torch cacti (*Cleistocactus strausii*), old man cacti (*Espostoa nana*), and giant chalk dudleya (*Dudleya brittonii*) stand out in a planter bed of black charcoal.

INTERIORS

There's a fine balance when designing interior plantscapes—rooms often feel cold or incomplete without plants, yet some rooms can feel suffocated by them. However, careful selections and a little restraint will yield spectacular results. Classic terracotta and unglazed pottery will never age, whereas plastics and bright colors can easily date a space and tire the viewer's eye. Observing the room's color scheme and furnishings, then selecting a specimen that compliments them is crucial, as is not to forget taking into consideration the scale and balance once the plant is chosen. Plants that can go dry between watering are bullet proof, so cacti, anthuriums, dracaenas, and sansevierias are a negligent plant lover's best friend.

Watering is an issue for plants 15 feet off the ground, so unthirsty plants like snake plants (*Sansevieria trifasciata*) and cacti like *Cleistocactus* get monthly waters. Here, they provide a graphic element to the rotunda of the store.

Cacti are featured in the entry planter at Heath Ceramics. Opposite, clockwise from top left: Plowmanii fruffles (*Anthurium plowmanii*) love indirect light and sporadic watering; a crested cactus watches over the kitchen; potted cacti in the living room; a yellow African candelabra (*Euphorbia ammak* 'Variegata') in a stone planter.

CONTAINER GARDENS

The last step of any exterior project is often the container selection and installation. And usually this is the point where things can fall apart due to busy arrangements and noxious colors that pull attention away from their surroundings. The key to successful planter design is to keep it simple. Plants have differing growth habits—arranging multiple specimens in a pot will look out of balance in a matter of months and will require constant replache best option is to plant only one type of specimen in each container. Container selection is also key—neutrals can match any season, so they make the best sense for long-term planters. Once planted, prune the plant over time to highlight its structure and form, and keep the soil from looking bare by covering it with a layer of decorative rock, sand, or stone.

Opposite: Crested myrtillocactus (*Myrtillocactus geometrizans cristata*) in the foreground shares a narrow balcony with potted *Furcraea macdougalii* and *Aloe barberae.*

Two potted beaked
yucca (*Yucca rostrata*)
are arranged in a
staggered formation
in a front entry of a
San Francisco home,
the twisted cabbage
tree (*Cussonia spicata*)
occupies the corner
at the door, and the
Galanter & Jones bench
and seat are heated.

An expertly placed mirror creates the illusion of infinite golden barrel cacti (*Echinocactus grusonii*), while a potted candelabra tree (*Euphorbia ingens*) leans against a wall and *Echeveria colorata* succulents fills a shallow bowl. Opposite: A collection of cacti creates a dramatic backdrop in this serene garden. A stately Bismarck palm (*Bismarckia nobilis*) holds court in the corner.

A trio of elephant ear (*Kalanchoe beharensis*), red pencil cactus (*Euphorbia tirucalli* 'Sticks on Fire,') and rainbow bush (*Portulacaria afra* 'Variegata'). Opposite, clockwise from top left: giant chalk Dudleya (*Dudleya brittonii*); spineless yucca (*Yucca elephantipes*); podocarpus (*Podocarpus elongatus* 'Monmal') and zebra haworthia (*Haworthia fasciata* 'Zebra Haworthia'); and tree Euphorbia (*Euphorbia lambii*) with naked elephant ear (*Kalanchoe beharensis* 'Nudum').

Clockwise, from top left: elephant ear (*Kalanchoe beharensis*); assorted cacti with century plant (*Agave Americana*), candelabra trees (*Euphorbia ingens*), and Mexican grass trees (*Dasylirion longissimum*) with *Aloe dichotoma*. Opposite: Sago palm (*Cycas revolute*) and spineless yucca (*Yucca elephantipes*).

The author in a garden
of his own design in
Menlo Park, California.
The rope balls are by
landscape architect
Topher Delaney.

ACKNOWLEDGMENTS

I have connected with so many wonderful and inspiring people who contributed their time and talents to this book, and I share in their pride seeing these beautiful projects together in this book. My photographer, and friend, Caitlin Atkinson, is a voice of reason and support, and without her, this book would not be possible. I also want to thank my partner, Jake Foley, my agent Carole Bidnick and my friends, Bradley Duncan, Samer Fawaz, David Godshall, Rob Jones, Judy Kameon, Lee Ledbetter, Ron and Louise Mann, Johanna Silver, and all the others I met along the way, who opened their homes and schedules to accommodate us and truly share a collective vision that I couldn't have imagined when I began this journey. I would also be remiss not to mention my mentor, Flora Grubb, who gave me my first real job in her nursery and has supported and let me grow in a way that only patient and loving plant people can. Lastly, I want to dedicate this book to my parents, especially to my father, George, who asked me what I wanted to do with my life on a boat ride around Lake Greenwood and when I said "I want to be a landscape designer" he encouraged me to put my heart into it. It will be thirteen years since we had that talk and he is no longer with us, but every garden I plant carries a memory of him in it.

RESOURCES

SONOMA HILL TOP
LANDSCAPE ARCHITECT: **Arterra Landscape Architects Architects @ www.arterrasf.com**
ARCHITECT: **Feldman Architecture @ www.feldmanarchitecture.com**

SAN ANSELMO RESIDENCE
LANDSCAPE ARCHITECT: **Ron Lutsko @ www.lutskoassociates.com**
ARCHITECT: **Charlie Barnett Assoc @ www.charliebarnettassoc.com**

BERNAL HEIGHTS RESIDENCE
LANDSCAPE DESIGN: **Daniel Nolan @ www.danielnolandesign.com**
ARCHITECT: **David Sternberg @ www.sternbergbenjamin.com**

MID PENINSULA GARDEN
LANDSCAPE DESIGN: **Daniel Nolan @ www.danielnolandesign.com**
ARCHITECT: **Matthew Mosey @ www.dumicanmosey.com**

CARMEL CLIFF HOUSE
LANDSCAPE AND ARCHITECT: **Ronn Mann @ www.ronmanndesign.com**

LOS PALMAS ESTATE
LANDSCAPE ARCHITECT: **Steve Martino @ www.stevemartino.net**

SADDLE PEAK
LANDSCAPE AND ARCHITECT: **Michael Sant @ www.santarchitects.com**

BEL AIR ANZIO
LANDSCAPE ARCHITECT: **Terremoto @ www.terremoto.la**

BEL AIR ESTATE
LANDSCAPE ARCHITECT: **Lisa Gimmy @ www.lglalandscape.com**

HANCOCK PARK HIDEAWAY
LANDSCAPE DESIGN: **Adam Sirak @ www.sirak.com**

HERMOSA PROJECT
LANDSCAPE ARCHITECT: **Rob Jones @ www.joneslandscapesla.com**
ARCHITECT: **Michael Lee @ www.mleearchitects.com**

PHOENIX OASIS
LANDSCAPE ARCHITECT: **Colwell Shelor @ www.colwellshelor.com**

DESERT RETREAT
LANDSCAPE DESIGN: **The Garden Gate @ www.landscapedesigntucson.com**
ARCHITECT: **Ibarra Rosano @ www.ibarrarosano.com**

CLOS PEGASE WINERY
LANDSCAPE DESIGN: **Daniel Nolan @ www.danielnolandesign.com**

SCRIBE WINERY
LANDSCAPE ARCHITECT: **Terremoto @ www.terremoto.la**

TONGVA PARK
LANDSCAPE ARCHITECT: **James Corner Field Operations @ www.fieldoperations.net**

ISABEL MARANT
LANDSCAPE DESIGN: **Judy Kameon @ www.elysianlandscapes.com**

MOHAWK WEST
LANDSCAPE ARCHITECT: **Terremoto @ www.terremoto.la**

OLMOS PARK PROJECT
LANDSCAPE AND ARCHITECT: **Lake Flato @ www.lakeflato.com**

LOS BALCONES
LANDSCAPE ARCHITECT: **Mark Word @ www.markworddesign.com**
ARCHITECT: **Mell Lawrence Architects @ www.melllawrencearchitects.com**

NEW ORLEANS MID-CENTURY
DESIGN: **Lee Ledbetter @ www.leeledbetter.com**

JOHNS ISLAND
DESIGN: **Jim Smeal and Alejandro Gonzalez**

PECKERWOOD GARDEN
LANDSCAPE DESIGN: **John Fairey**
ARCHITECT: **Gerald Maffei @ www.geraldlmaffei.com**

ALYS BEACH COMMUNITY
LANDSCAPE AND ARCHITECT:
Duany Plater-Zyberk @ www.dpz.com